Cataloging-in-Publication Data

Names: James, Ryan.
Title: Harvesters on the job / Ryan James.
Description: Buffalo, NY : Norwood House Press, 2026. | Series: Big machines for big jobs | Includes glossary and index.
Identifiers: ISBN 9781978573901 (pbk.) | ISBN 9781978573918 (library bound) | ISBN 9781978573925 (ebook)
Subjects: LCSH: Harvesting machinery--Juvenile literature. | Agricultural machinery--Juvenile literature.
Classification: LCC S695.J359 2026 | DDC 681.'7631--dc23

Published in 2026 by
Norwood House Press
2544 Clinton Street
Buffalo, NY 14224

Copyright © 2026 Norwood House Press
Designer: Rhea Magaro
Editor: Kim Thompson

Photo credits: Cover, p. 1 Radu Cadar/Shutterstock.com; p. 3 Kirti Bhole/Shutterstock.com; p. 5 Scharfsinn/Shutterstock.com; p. 6 Solid photos/Shutterstock.com; p. 7 smereka/Shutterstock.com; p. 9, 15 vlalukinv/Shutterstock.com; p. 10 roibu/Shutterstock.com; p. 12, 13 Sergey Dudikov/Shutterstock.com; p. 14 Claudia HarmsWarlies/Shutterstock.com; p. 17 Hryshchyshen Serhii/Shutterstock.com; p. 18 Fotokostic/Shutterstock.com; p. 19 bbernard/Shutterstock.com; p. 21 Dusan Petkovic/Shutterstock.com;

All rights reserved. No part of this book may be reproduced in any form without permission in writing from the publisher, except by a reviewer.

Printed in the United States of America

Some of the images in this book illustrate individuals who are models. The depictions do not imply actual situations or events.

CPSIA compliance information: Batch #CSNHP26: For further information contact Norwood House Press at 1-800-237-9932.

TABLE OF CONTENTS

Parts of a Harvester 4

What Does a Harvester Do? 8

Harvester Safety 16

Harvesters in Action 20

Glossary 22

Thinking Questions 23

Index 24

About the Author 24

PARTS OF A HARVESTER

Harvesters are big machines. Many harvesters have four wheels.

A harvester has a cab. The driver sits there. The header and rotor are in front of the cab.

The **grain** tank is behind the cab.

Some tanks are beside the harvester.

WHAT DOES A HARVESTER DO?

Harvesters work on farms. They **harvest** farm **crops**. They move through rows in the fields. They cut down plants. They **separate** the food from the rest of the plant.

The header has sharp **blades**. They spin quickly. They cut plant stems.

The rotor is a **cylinder**. It spins. It separates the grain from the leaves and stems. The grain moves upward. It is stored in the grain tank.

There are different kinds of harvesters. Forage harvesters make **silage**. It is food for **livestock**.

Corn harvesters collect ears of corn. Soybean harvesters harvest **soybeans**.

HARVESTER SAFETY

Stay safe around harvesters so nobody gets hurt. Do not touch any sharp parts. An adult should always be with you.

When a harvester is working, stay out of its path. This lets the harvester keep going.

Do not bend the plants. Leave them alone so the harvester can pick them.

HARVESTERS IN ACTION

Harvesters are **vehicles** on the job.

They harvest food for you to eat!

GLOSSARY

blades (blades): flat, sharp-edged tools for cutting

crops (krahps): plants grown on a farm for food, such as wheat, corn, and soybeans

cylinder (SIL-uhn-dur): a round tube that turns inside a machine

grain (grayn): the seeds of wheat, oats, and other plants which are used to make cereal, bread, and other foods

harvest (HAHR-vist): to gather crops from a field

livestock (LIVE-stahk): animals raised on farms, such as cows and chickens

separate (SEP-uh-rate): to take things apart or pull things away from each other

silage (SYE-lij): chopped-up plants that are stored in a silo and used to feed animals

soybeans (SOI-beenz): seeds that grow in pods on bushy plants and that are used to make oil and other foods

vehicles (VEE-i-kuhlz): machines used to move people or things from one place to another

THINKING QUESTIONS

1. What is the job of a harvester?

2. How is each type of harvester different from the others?

3. How does a harvester use blades?

4. How can you stay safe around a harvester?

5. Why are harvesters important?

INDEX

corn 15

crops 8

driver 6

food 8, 14, 20

grain 7, 13

header 6, 11

livestock 14

plants 8, 11, 19

rotor 6, 13

soybeans 15

ABOUT THE AUTHOR

Ryan James lives in the mountains of North Carolina where he goes hiking with his dog Bailey. He loves fly fishing, visiting farms in the area, and picking fresh produce. He has always enjoyed writing and wrote his first book as a teenager.